Edible Object Talks

That Teach About
Jesus

by
Susan L. Lingo

Standard®
PUBLISHING
Bringing The Word to Life
Cincinnati, Ohio

Dedication

How sweet are your words to my taste,
sweeter than honey to my mouth!
Psalm 119:103

Credits
Produced by Susan L. Lingo, Bright Ideas Books™
Illustrated by Paula Becker
Cover design by Liz Howe

12 11 10 09 08 07 06   12 11 10 9 8 7 6
ISBN-13: 978-0-7847-1184-2
ISBN-10: 0-7847-1184-4

THE MENU

WHAT DO THE BiBLE, TORTiLLAS, TiCKLED TUMMiES, AND HAPPY TEACHERS HAVE iN COMMON?

Powerful Bible truths that are as nutritious to learn as they are fun to eat!

Edible Object Talks That Teach About Jesus is filled with twenty-five motivating, life-changing biblical messages served up in neat-to-eat treats that will help your kids devour and digest God's Word—and leave them shouting for seconds! Each memorable message introduces an important truth from the life of Jesus for kids to nurture in their lives, such as loving our enemies, sharing, witnessing, calming fears, and encouraging others. Kids interact with each message by reading from the Bible, discussing the importance of each truth, and preparing simple snacks as tasty reminders of Bible truths. Kids come away from these message munchies filled with

- memorable reminders of God's Word,
- an awareness of Jesus' truth for their lives,
- life-changing challenges for the upcoming week, and
- a sense of community and teamwork.

Use these neat-to-eat treats as motivating object talks, snack-time fun with a focus, or as super VBS together-times. Make every moment with your kids count as you present dynamic devotions they'll devour and memorable messages they'll digest!

(Please remember to check for possible food allergies before beginning *any* food activity.)

SOME CHANGE, PLEASE!

OOD FOR THOUGHT

Jesus can change us if we accept his love. *(Luke 19:1-8; 2 Corinthians 5:17)*

IMPLE INGREDIENTS

You'll need a Bible, carrots, plastic spoons, four mixing bowls and spoons, a pitcher of hot water, a bag of ice, a clear plastic cup for each child, and two boxes each of lime-flavored gelatin and lemon-flavored gelatin. For extra fun, you may also want whipped cream topping and gold foil-wrapped chocolate coins.

Before class, slice several carrots into edible "coins" to add to the gelatin during the object talk.

EVOURING THE MESSAGE

Form four groups and hand each a bowl, a spoon, and a box of powdered gelatin. Set a pitcher of very hot water nearby and place the remaining ingredients on a table. Have kids empty the powdered gelatin into their bowls, then ask them to describe what they see. Say: **The gelatin in your bowls is powdery and dry, isn't it? Let's see what we can do to change the dry gelatin into something completely different!**

Pour a cup full of hot water into each bowl and let kids take turns stirring to dissolve the gelatin. As they stir, say: **Changing some things can be very good. We change our socks when they're dirty, we change our habits when they're unhealthy, and we change tires when they're flat. Did you know that we can change our hearts and lives, too? As we continue making this neat treat to eat, let's learn how Jesus helped someone change his heart and life for the better. And watch carefully because we'll be changing our gelatin, too!**

Add a cup of ice cubes to each bowl and have kids stir the ice as you retell the story of Zacchaeus from Luke 19:1-8. Be sure to explain how Zacchaeus changed his life after receiving Jesus' love and forgiveness and then demonstrated the change by giving back the people's money and more. As kids continue to stir, the gelatin should thicken greatly. Add a few more ice cubes to each bowl if needed. As kids finish dissolving the ice, ask:

- 🍎 **How did Zacchaeus's life become changed?**
- 🍎 **In what ways did Jesus help Zacchaeus change?**
- 🍎 **How did Zacchaeus show he was changed?**
- 🍎 **What are changes we make in our lives when we love Jesus?**

Spoon layers of the thickened gelatin, alternating the flavors, into the clear plastic cups. Then add several carrot coins to each. If you desire, place a dollop of whipped cream on top and a chocolate coin in the topping.

Say: **We changed the gelatin by adding water and ice, and we could see the gelatin change and thicken as we stirred it. Zacchaeus became changed when Jesus gave him love and forgiveness. To show he was changed, Zacchaeus repaid everyone with coins. As we munch our treats, let's think of ways we can show others we have been changed through Jesus' love and forgiveness during the coming week.**

Suggest ways such as saying kinder words, being more helpful, sharing with others, praying and reading the Bible, and telling others about Jesus. End by reading aloud 2 Corinthians 5:17 and by sharing a prayer asking Jesus' help in living changed lives, then thanking him for his love and forgiveness. Let kids take their cups and chocolate coins (if you used them) home as reminders of the object talk.

ICE-CREAM BOATS AFLOAT

OOD FOR THOUGHT

Jesus helps calm our fears. (*Joshua 1:9; Matthew 8:23-27*)

IMPLE INGREDIENTS

You'll need a Bible, chilled root beer, an ice-cream scoop, resealable plastic bags, drinking straws, ice cream, and maraschino cherries.

DEVOURING THE MESSAGE

Hand each child a plastic bag. Ask kids to tell about things that make them afraid, such as storms, being alone, or even the dark. Say: **We all have different fears that cause us to worry or lose focus. Jesus knows we have fears, but he also wants us to know that he's right here helping us and staying close! Let's learn about the way Jesus calmed his disciples' fears one stormy night at sea as we make delicious snacks.**

Say: **One night, Jesus and his disciples were sailing on the Sea of Galilee. It was dark—even the water seemed dark as it reflected the nighttime sky.** Fill each plastic bag half full of root beer. Have kids hold the bags closed and gently rock them to make waves as you continue: **The waves were gentle on the sea as the little boat sailed along, floating on the waves.** Add cherry "boats" to the plastic bags and hold them closed.

Say: **The boat rocked and rolled over the waves, and Jesus soon fell asleep. Everything felt safe and secure. Then all of a sudden, storm clouds rolled in!** Add a scoop of ice-cream "cloud" to each bag, then have kids seal the plastic bags securely. **A mighty storm beat down upon the sea! Lightning and thunder crashed and boomed, and the waves became frothy and huge!** Jiggle the plastic bags to make large waves. **Would the boat stay afloat? Would they all drown in the storm? The disciples were so afraid! They ran to wake Jesus. "How can you sleep? We all may drown! How can you sleep when we're sinking on down?" Jesus stood at the bow and commanded the wind and the waves to be still—and they obeyed.**

TIDBITS

Kids might enjoy knowing that the Sea of Galilee was really a twelve-mile-long lake! Storms often came upon the lake in minutes, causing boats to sink and sailors to shiver with fear!

Stop shaking the bags and wait for the cherries to calmly float. Then say: **The storm stopped. The waves stilled. And the boat stayed afloat. Jesus stopped the storm, and the disciples were no longer afraid. Who was this, they wondered, who could control the sea and storms? They had learned that Jesus is power-ful enough to calm any storm and any fears!**

Hand each child a drinking straw and let kids open one slit in their plastic bags to slide the straws through. As kids sip their snacks, read aloud Joshua 1:9, then ask:

🍎 **Why were the disciples smart to call upon Jesus in their fear?**

🍎 **In what ways did Jesus' help show his love for the disciples? for us?**

🍎 **How does it help to know that Jesus is always with us, calming our fears?**

🍎 **What fears of our own can we give to Jesus to deal with?**

Say: **Sometimes our fears make us feel like we're in a bad storm! We might even wonder if we can stay afloat! But just as Jesus calmed the wind and waves** for the disciples, he can calm our fears and help when we have worries. **Look at the cherry boats on your seas. See how they bounce and float? Jesus' caring love does the same for us—it keeps us bouncing along when we trust him! We'll never sink with Jesus near!**

When the last of the root-beer floats have been sipped, have kids hold their maraschino cherries. Say: **Let's end with a prayer. We'll thank Jesus for his love and help. But don't eat your cheery cherries until the end!** Pray: **Dear Lord, thank you for your loving help. It's so good to know that we can give our troubles to you and you will calm us. When we trust you to help, we're as cheery as cherries! Amen.** Let children pop the cherries into their mouths to enjoy.

End by encouraging kids to prepare these neat treats for their families and friends as cool reminders that Jesus calms our fears!

FiSH AND LoAVES

OOD FOR THOUGHT

Jesus has love enough for everyone. *(John 6:1-14; Ephesians 3:17-19)*

IMPLE INGREDIENTS

You'll need a Bible, soft flour tortillas, plastic knives, tuna salad, napkins, and a wicker bread basket.

Before class, prepare a large bowl of tuna salad. Use your favorite recipe or simply mix together drained tuna, mayonnaise, and a bit of pickle relish. Be sure you have two flour tortillas for each child.

EVOURING THE MESSAGE

Have kids form groups of two or three and hand each child a napkin and a flour tortilla. Challenge kids to tear the tortillas into as many pieces on the napkins as possible in two minutes.

After the tortillas are shredded, say: **Look at the food you've divided on your napkins. Is there enough food there to share with the whole class? How about with our entire church? What about with one hundred people? That would seem impossible, wouldn't it? Yet Jesus did something even more amazing than that! He fed an entire crowd of five thousand people with just five loaves of bread and two fish. Wow! Now that's stretching the food budget! But Jesus performed that miracle, and there was even enough food left over to fill twelve baskets!** Invite children to nibble their tortillas as you read aloud John 6:1-14. Then ask:

 🍎 **Why do you think Jesus wanted to feed such a big crowd?**

 🍎 **How was Jesus' sharing of the fish and loaves a demonstration of his love? of his power?**

 🍎 **What can we learn about sharing with others from Jesus' miracle? What can we learn about loving others?**

Say: **Jesus wanted to feed those hungry people because he loved them, and Jesus provided more than enough to go around! In fact, Jesus has more than enough love to share with everyone—and he shares his love freely. We can learn from Jesus' miracle of the fish and loaves that we have enough of God's love to share with everyone we know—and even those we don't know!** Read aloud Ephesians 3:17-19, then ask:

 🍎 **What are ways to share our love?**

 🍎 **How can we share love with others we know? with people we don't know?**

Say: **Jesus multiplied and shared food so there was enough for everyone. Jesus also had enough love for everyone. Let's make Fish and Loaves tortillas to remind us that we have love enough to share with five people or maybe even five thousand when we have Jesus' love helping us!**

Show kids how to spread tuna salad on a flour tortilla, then roll the tortilla up and place it in the bread basket. When all the Fish and Loaves tortillas are in the basket, have children find a place to sit, then say: **Before Jesus shared food with the five thousand, he prayed and gave thanks. Let's share a prayer thanking Jesus for his love that's large enough for everyone.** Pray: **Dear Lord, thank you for your amazing love. Please help us share our love with others as you've shared your love with us. Amen.**

Pass out the Fish and Loaves tortillas. As you enjoy them, visit about ways you can share love with others this week, such as praying for them, speaking encouraging words, or even telling them about Jesus' perfect love. If there's time, prepare Fish and Loaves tortillas for another class and share with them as you retell the story of Jesus feeding the five thousand. Remind everyone that Jesus has enough love to go around—and then some!

WAIT FOR THE DATE

OOD FOR THOUGHT

Jesus will return in his own time. *(John 14:1-3; 1 Thessalonians 4:16; Hebrews 10:35-37)*

IMPLE INGREDIENTS

You'll need a Bible, napkins, pitted dates, plastic spoons, cream cheese, and leaves of endive lettuce. If you'd like a special touch, add two cans of drained palm hearts.

Before class, wash the lettuce (and drain and pat dry the palm hearts if you desire to use them). Remember, a unique taste treat can make a memorable message even more unforgettable! Partially cut each date lengthwise. Make sure you have two dates (and one palm heart) for each child. Deliver this meaningful message around Easter time.

EVOURING THE MESSAGE

Place snack ingredients on a table and ask kids to tell about things that are hard to wait for, such as birthdays, Christmas, vacation time, or even the first day of school. Say: **When we're waiting for a special time or event, it's often hard to have patience! Birthdays, holidays, and other exciting times are great—but not the wait! Where is our patience?** Hand each child a napkin and two dates, then say: **These are very patient little fruits. Did you know that dates grow on palm trees and that it takes five years to grow a date? That's a long time to wait!** Hand out the lettuce leaves and say: **Palm leaves are what the people waved when Jesus entered Jerusalem for the Passover Feast before he was crucified and risen. It takes many more years to grow palm fronds long enough to wave!** Have kids wave the lettuce leaves and say, "Hosanna! Hosanna!"

Have kids place the lettuce leaves (and palm hearts) on the napkins, then lay the dates on the lettuce. Say: **Dates and date palm trees were important to the people who lived during Jesus' time, but it took great patience to wait for the right time to pick them. Dates, holidays, and birthdays are all important to** wait for, but Jesus promised us something much more important and worth waiting for. Jesus promised to return to earth! But the tricky part is, we don't know the time or day. Listen to what the Bible says about Jesus' return. Read aloud John 14:1-3; Hebrews 10:35-37; and 1 Thessalonians 4:16. Then ask:

🍎 How do we know Jesus will return?

🍎 Why is it important to have patience?

🍎 What can we do to make waiting for Jesus an even more valuable time?

Say: We might wait for Jesus' return for five years like the dates, or maybe fifty or five hundred years! But we know that Jesus will return because that's what he promised! And we can wait for the date with patience and a serving attitude. In other words, we can fill our lives with a work-while-we-wait attitude of helping others and serving Christ! Let's fill our dates as we explore ways to fill our days being patient!

As kids stuff cream cheese into their dates, encourage them to name ways we can serve Jesus while we wait for his return. Suggest doing kind things for others, reading the Bible, learning God's Word, and praying. After the dates are prepared, share a prayer asking for Jesus' help in being patient as you wait for his return. Enjoy the snack, then challenge kids to prepare this tasty treat for families and friends as they tell about Jesus' return and our patient wait-for-the-date attitudes!

OOD FOR THOUGHT

Jesus wants us to love and rely on the Trinity. *(Matthew 28:19; John 10:38; 2 Corinthians 13:14)*

IMPLE INGREDIENTS

You'll need a Bible, napkins, a large tray, a banana for each child plus one extra, and three bowls each containing one of the following toppings: strawberry, butterscotch, and marshmallow creme.

Before class, fill three bowls with the toppings, then place the bowls on a large tray to catch any drips or spills. Be sure the bananas aren't overly ripe!

DEVOURING THE MESSAGE

Gather kids and hold up an unpeeled banana. Say: **It looks as if I have only one banana here, doesn't it? But I really have three bananas in one! Watch!** Peel the banana half way, then slowly poke your finger into the top of the banana. It will separate into three segments. Say: **Wow! Three bananas in one! Jesus teaches us about another three-in-one called the Trinity—the Father who is God, the Son who is Jesus, and the Holy Spirit. Let's see what the Bible says about the three-in-one and one-in-three Trinity!** Read aloud Matthew 28:19; John 10:38; and 2 Corinthians 13:14. Then ask:

🍎 **Who is in the Trinity? How is each equally wonderful and worthy of our love and praise?**

🍎 **How does it help to know that God, Jesus, and the Holy Spirit are all loving and helping us?**

🍎 **In what ways can we trust the Father, Son, and Holy Spirit more?**

Say: **We can trust the Trinity—or Godhead—to help, love, guide, and teach us. Let's learn more about the Trinity as we enjoy making special banana splits!**

Hand out the bananas and napkins. Invite kids to peel their bananas half way, then poke their fingers into the tops to make three sections. Dip one section into the marshmallow and say: **White is for our loving Father who is God. God created us, taught us how to love and obey him, and sent his Son, Jesus, so we could be forgiven from our sins.** Dip another section of banana into the strawberry topping, then say: **Red is the color of Jesus, God's Son. Jesus showed us how to love God and others. He also died so we could be forgiven and live at peace with God.** Dip the last section of banana into the butterscotch topping and say: **And yellow is the color of the Holy Spirit, whose fire helps us be brave and serve Jesus. Jesus sent us the Holy Spirit to be a special friend and helper. What a team we have! And Jesus wants us to accept and rely on our holy team every day of our lives!**

Before we nibble our banana splits, let's offer a prayer thanking the Trinity for loving and helping us. Pray: **Dear Lord, thank you for providing for us in every way from love and forgiveness to help and teaching! In the name of the Father, Son, and Holy Spirit, we love and thank you! Amen.**

As kids enjoy dipping and munching their banana splits, encourage them to name ways each member of the Trinity touches our lives. Point out how each loves, helps, and teaches us. Explain your church's view of the Trinity and consider inviting a church leader to share with your kids and answer questions they might have.

FABULOUS FISHNETS

OOD FOR THOUGHT

Jesus can do anything! *(Luke 1:37; John 21:4-8)*

IMPLE INGREDIENTS

You'll need a Bible, small clear cups, spoons, paper plates, fish-shaped candies, black permanent markers, and a tub of thickened blue gelatin.

Before class, prepare a tub of thickened blue gelatin to make a "sea." Use one large box of blue gelatin for every six kids. Be sure the gelatin is thickened but not set. Stir in a bag of fish-shaped candies. Keep an extra bag of candy fish for later in the message.

EVOURING THE MESSAGE

Set the tub of blue gelatin and fish-shaped candies beside you, but don't let anyone peek inside! Gather kids and ask them to tell about things that seem impossible to do, such as making the rain stop during a picnic, lifting a mountain, or memorizing an encyclopedia.

Then say: **There are so many things that seem impossible for us to do. Sometimes we can feel so frustrated when it's impossible to fix a broken toy in a snap or make fish jump into nets to feed hungry people. But we know someone who can do these things plus a whole lot more! We know that Jesus can do anything! Let's learn about a time Jesus helped his friends by performing an awesome miracle. We'll be pretend fishermen in our boats.**

13

Have kids sit in groups of four on the floor and hand each group a marker and clear cups. **You'll need fishing nets, so draw lines on your cups for make-believe nets while I tell you what happened that special day.**

After Jesus had risen from the grave, his disciples went fishing on the sea. It was nighttime, and they threw their nets into the water but caught nothing. All night long they fished, but by morning no one had caught a single fish! Jesus stood on the beach, but his friends didn't recognize him. Jesus told them to toss their nets on the right side of the boat.

Have kids hold their cups to the right, then say: **They obeyed—and guess what happened? Let's see!** Have kids close their eyes and dip their cups into the tub of gelatin and candy fish. Then hand them paper plates to catch any drips. **They caught more fish than could fit in their nets! Then the disciples recognized Jesus. Why? Because they knew that only Jesus can do anything! How else could they have caught all those fish?**

As children spoon up their miraculous catches, read aloud John 21:4-8 and Luke 1:37, then ask:

🍎 **In what ways do Jesus' miracles demonstrate his love?**

🍎 **How does knowing that Jesus can do anything help us trust him more? rely on him? praise him?**

🍎 **In what ways did obeying Jesus help the disciples? How does obeying Jesus help us?**

🍎 **How does knowing that Jesus is all-powerful help us when we have troubles? when we're sad or lonely?**

Say: **Knowing that Jesus can do anything gives us real comfort! We can trust that even when things look hopeless, Jesus can help. All we have to do is ask him, trust him, and obey him! Isn't that wonderful? That means we can trust Jesus and pray for his guidance and help whenever we need it—and know that nothing is too big or too hard for Jesus to take care of in his own way.** Hand each child a fish-shaped candy and say: **Let's close with a fun rhyme to remind us that Jesus is all-powerful.**

Repeat the following rhyme, then have kids pop the candy fish into their mouths.

The disciples fished all night through,
Caught no fish and felt so blue!
But Jesus came to help them all,
Across the sea they heard him call:
"Toss in your nets!"—then glip, glop, glup—
They caught the fish and ate them up!
Now, like the disciples, we can sing,
Jesus can do anything!

FANCY DIPPERS

OOD FOR THOUGHT

Jesus wants us to be baptized. *(Matthew 3:13-17; Acts 2:38, 39; 4:12)*

IMPLE INGREDIENTS

You'll need a Bible, paper plates, fancy toothpicks (available at party supply stores), plastic bowls, ice-cream toppings such as chocolate and butterscotch, and fresh fruits such as strawberries, bananas, apples, grapes, and pineapple.

Before class, wash and cut the fruit into chunks. Kids will be dipping the fruit into toppings much like fondue, so be sure the fruit is chunky enough to stay on toothpicks. If your class is young, consider using pretzel sticks instead of fancy toothpicks to dip the fruits.

EVOURING THE MESSAGE

Place the paper plates, toothpicks, fruits, and bowls of topping on a table. Gather kids, dip a piece of fruit in chocolate and say: **When this fruit was dipped, it became covered, didn't it? The Bible teaches us about another type of dipping where we become covered by God's grace. Let's read about it from the Bible.**

Read aloud Matthew 3:13-17, then say: **Jesus was baptized when he went to the Jordan River and was covered with water by John the Baptist—and God was pleased. The baptism symbolized cleanness and being ready for God's forgiveness. Jesus had nothing to ask forgiveness for, but we do. And when we're baptized, it shows we're sorry for our sins, we're ready to accept Jesus into our lives, and we want to be covered with God's grace. The word baptism comes from the Greek word** *baptizo,* **which means "to dip or immerse." And just as a piece of fruit**

TIDBITS

Kids might like to know that fruit was a delicious part of the Jewish diet and included dates, figs, grapes, and pome-granates. Fruits were often dipped into a sweet paste made from crushed almonds.

dipped in topping becomes covered with sweetness, we become covered with God's sweet grace when we're baptized. Read aloud Acts 2:38, 39; 4:12, then ask:

🍎 Why does Jesus want us to be baptized? Why is God pleased when we're baptized?

🍎 How does baptism demonstrate our love and obedience for Jesus?

🍎 Why is it important to be covered by God's grace?

Distribute the paper plates and invite children to dip and enjoy eating pieces of fruit. As you enjoy your dippers, discuss the importance of baptism and how your church chooses to baptize. You may wish to invite a church leader in for the discussion and to share your snacks.

End by saying: Jesus was baptized, and he wants us to do the same. In fact, Jesus told us to go into the world and baptize others in the name of the Father, the Son, and the Holy Spirit. When we repent of our sins and are baptized, we become covered by God's grace, mercy, approval, and unending love! What a sweet treat!

ASSEMBLY-LINE SNACKS

OOD FOR THOUGHT

Jesus sent us a special helper! *(John 14:15-17, 26; 15:26)*

IMPLE INGREDIENTS

You'll need a Bible, napkins, a large tray, plastic spoons, a jar of pizza sauce, shredded cheese, a package of sliced pepperoni, and a box of small round crackers.

EVOURING THE MESSAGE

Set up the snack ingredients on a long table in the following order: napkins, crackers, pizza sauce, cheese, pepperoni, large tray. Set the plastic spoons by the sauce and cheese. Form six groups of two or three children each. If your class is large, set up a second table and ingredients. Be sure kids have clean hands, then direct each group to stand by a different ingredient at the table, from the napkins to the tray.

Explain that you'll be making pizza rounds in an assembly line and that everyone is a helper. Tell kids that the napkin people will hand a napkin to the cracker people, who will add a cracker to the napkin, then pass it along to the sauce group. The sauce group will spread a bit of sauce on the cracker, then send it to the cheese people, who will add a bit of shredded cheese. Next, the cracker passes to the pepperoni people, who can drop a pepperoni slice on top, then to the tray group to arrange the crackers on the tray. Tell kids they have five minutes to prepare all the snacks!

After five minutes, call time. Gather kids and ask:

🍎 **What was it like doing this job in only a few minutes?**

🍎 **How did it encourage you to have many helpers?**

🍎 **Could you have completed this task on time without help? Explain.**

Say: **Sometimes we have tough jobs to do and need help. As Christians, there are many jobs we do that require special help. Missionaries need help bringing God's Word to foreign countries. Pastors need help in running their churches. And we need help in serving others and telling people about Jesus. It's a good thing Jesus sent us a special helper! Let's find out who that helper is and how he helps us.** Read aloud John 14:15-17, 26; 15:26. Then ask:

🍎 **Why do you think Jesus sent the Holy Spirit to help us?**

🍎 **How did Jesus demonstrate his love when he sent the Holy Spirit?**

🍎 **How can we let the Holy Spirit help us more fully?**

🍎 **What are things the Holy Sprit can help us do?**

Say: **Jesus sent us the Holy Spirit as our special comforter, friend, and helper. The Holy Spirit helps us do what Jesus would do if he were on earth. Through the help of the Holy Spirit, we can serve one another, love each other, and offer help to those in need. Just as we helped each other make snacks, the Holy Spirit gives us a mighty helping hand! Now let's give each other another helping hand as we serve our treats to another room and share with them the great news about our special helper, the Holy Spirit!**

Encourage your children to serve the pizza snacks to kids in another class, then share with them the snacks and a prayer thanking Jesus for sending us the Holy Spirit to be our handy helper!

TiDBiTS

This object talk is wonderful to share with another class after the snacks are prepared. The recipe feeds about twenty children, so adjust it accordingly.

RECIPE FOR LOVE

OOD FOR THOUGHT

Jesus wants us to tell the good news about his love and forgiveness!
(Matthew 28:19, 20; Romans 10:15)

IMPLE INGREDIENTS

You'll need a Bible, slips of paper, pens, 1/4 cup flour, 2 tablespoons sugar, 1 tablespoon cornstarch, 2 tablespoons cooking oil, 1 egg white, 1 tablespoon water, and nonstick cooking spray. You'll also need paper towels, powdered sugar, several spoons, a metal spatula, and an electric skillet.

Before class, mix the cookie ingredients in a bowl, adding the water last. (Do not add the powdered sugar.) The mixture should have a thick, batter-like consistency. This recipe makes about eight cookies, so increase the recipe to fit your class size. Cut 2-by-3-inch slips of paper, one for each cookie. If your class is large, use two electric skillets and enlist the help of an adult volunteer for the second skillet.

EVOURING THE MESSAGE

Set the can of cooking spray beside the electric skillet and heat the skillet to medium-high. Keep the skillet out of kids' reach for now. Ask one or two kids to tell about a favorite recipe or snack they like to make or eat. Then ask:

🍎 **How is telling someone the ingredients in a recipe sharing with them? helping them? teaching them?**

🍎 **In what ways is telling someone about Jesus like sharing an important recipe for love and forgiveness?**

🍎 **Why is the good news about Jesus the most important thing we can share? How can it change our lives? someone else's life?**

Say: **There are many great recipes for snacks, nutritious meals, and more. And sharing these recipes is not only helpful and informative, it can be fun, too. That's how it is with telling others about the special recipe for love and forgiveness with Jesus as the main ingredient! Although lots of recipes are tasty, Jesus' recipe for**

love and forgiveness is life-changing! That means telling others about Jesus can change our lives and others' lives, giving us hope, help, and even eternal life! Let's read what God's Word says about telling others the good news about Jesus. Ask a volunteer to read aloud Matthew 28:19, 20 and Romans 10:15. Then ask:

🍎 **What are things you can tell others about Jesus?**

🍎 **How does the Lord help us share the good news about Jesus?**

🍎 **Who can you tell about Jesus this week?**

Hand out slips of paper and pens and invite kids to write on the papers one thing they'd tell someone about Jesus. Suggestions might include that Jesus offers forgiveness, that Jesus calms our fears, or that Jesus teaches us how to love others.

Collect the papers, then spray the skillet with cooking spray and have kids spoon or pour a large tablespoon of cookie batter onto the skillet. Fry the flat cookies for three minutes, then flip them over and fry an additional minute. When the cookies are browned, place them on paper towels to drain. After a few seconds, place a slip of paper on each cookie and fold the cookie in half. Sprinkle the warm treats with powdered sugar. Respray the skillet after each use.

Pass out the cookies and let kids read aloud the mighty messages. Share the recipe, then challenge kids to make these cookies at home and present their tasty "tract treats" to friends to share the good news about Jesus!

OOD FOR THOUGHT

Jesus gives us new life. *(John 10:10; Ephesians 4:22-24; 5:8-11)*

IMPLE INGREDIENTS

You'll need a Bible, celery stalks, softened strawberry cream cheese, three-ring pretzels, raisins, plastic knives, and paper plates.

Before class, clean and cut a 6-inch celery stalk for each child. Be sure you have several plastic knives.

DEVOURING THE MESSAGE

Have kids form pairs or trios and hand each person a paper plate and celery stalk. Hand each group a plastic knife, then instruct kids to stuff the celery stalks with softened cream cheese. As kids work, tell them that they're making pretend cocoons, then ask what cocoons are and how they represent change. Make comments such as "When caterpillars are in cocoons, they change into butterflies" and "Cocoons seem so dark and dead but are really full of new life and change."

When the celery stalks are filled, say: **We see signs of new life and change all around us in the spring. Baby birds are born, then change and grow to be adults who can fly. New buds change into flowers and leaves. And caterpillars change into butterflies and emerge from dark cocoons. The world is full of new life and change in the springtime. But did you know we can have new life all year long when we love and accept Jesus into our lives? The Bible tells us about the special changes inside us when we have new life in Jesus.**

Read aloud John 10:10 and Ephesians 4:22-24; 5:8-11. Then ask:

🍎 **Why do we need new lives in Christ? What was wrong with our old lives?**

🍎 **What kinds of changes do we experience in new life with Jesus?**

🍎 **How can we help others have new lives in Christ?**

Have kids add raisin eyes at one end of the celery stalks as you say: **We change when we have new life in Christ. When we accept Jesus into our lives, we suddenly see clearer. We keep our eyes on Jesus and trust him more fully in our new lives.** Add broken pretzel antennas to the cream cheese above the raisin eyes and say: **New life in Jesus means hearing God more clearly. It also means we obey and listen to God's will in our lives.**

Stick two three-ringed pretzels to the sides of the celery stalk as "wings." Then say: **New life in Jesus also means we have the courage to fly high and accomplish many wonderful things! It means we can serve Jesus in awesome ways by helping and giving to others. Look at your butterflies and think of all the wonderful things we experience when we know, love, and follow Jesus! Now let's share a prayer thanking Jesus for the gift of new life in him.**

Pray: **Dear Jesus, thank you for loving us and for offering us new life in you. We're so happy that our old lives of sin and shame are gone when we accept you! Help us live our new lives serving and loving you. Amen.**

As kids enjoy nibbling their edible butterflies, have them brainstorm lists of what our lives were like before Jesus and what they're like now. Encourage kids to complete the statement: "In our old lives we (blank), but now we (blank)." For example, you might say, "In our old lives we said unkind words, but now we speak encouraging words." If there's time, write down the sentences kids make, then display them on a bulletin board for everyone to read and enjoy. Add paper butterflies around the edges and a colorful crepe-paper border.

FiSH iN THE SAND

OOD FOR THOUGHT

Jesus taught us how to encourage others. *(Hebrews 10:23, 24; 13:1, 2)*

IMPLE INGREDIENTS

You'll need a Bible, several colors of tube icing, paper towels, and a granola bar for each child.

EVOURING THE MESSAGE

Place the granola bars and tube icing on the table. Gather kids and have them say hello and greet each person. Then say: **It's nice to greet friends, isn't it? And there are so many ways to greet them, too! We can say hello with words, a handshake, a pat on the back, a hug, and even a kiss if we know them very well! How do you feel when someone takes the time to greet you?**

Allow kids time to tell their ideas, then say: **Not long after Jesus' death and resurrection, Christians began meeting to pray, honor, and teach others about Christ and to encourage one another. But because there were many people who didn't like Christians, they had to be careful when meeting or greeting one another. It would have been much easier to ignore their Christian friends,** but Jesus' followers knew that Jesus wants us to encourage one another and stick together. Let's see what the Bible says about encouraging one another. Read aloud Hebrews 10:23, 24; 13:1, 2. Then ask:

🍎 Why is it important to encourage our fellow Christians?

🍎 How does encouragement help us when we're lonely? afraid? have worries?

🍎 In what ways does encouraging other Christians strengthen their faith? our own faith?

🍎 What are encouraging things we can say to one another?

Say: **Those first Christians needed a lot of encouragement from each other. But if they openly greeted one another or spoke about Jesus, they ran the risk of being tossed in jail. How do you sup-**  **pose they greeted one another or left encouraging messages to others who loved Jesus? They drew pictures in the sand! They drew simple pictures of fish because Jesus taught Christians to be fishers of men. When a Christian met another Christian, they would quietly greet each other by drawing fish in the sand or dirt. It was a comfort and an encouragement to know there were other Christians teaching and serving. And Jesus wants us to be comforters and encouragers of fellow Christians, too. When we greet other members of God's family or speak encouraging words to them, we're telling them we love Jesus! And when we encourage others, we serve Jesus at the same time.**

Hand each child a paper towel and a granola bar. Have kids use icing to make simple fish shapes on their bars to represent the fish drawn in the sand by the early Christians. Then challenge kids to think of other symbols that represent their love for Jesus and draw them on the granola bars. Suggestions might be a heart for love, a dove for peace, a triangle for the Trinity, or a sun representing God's Son. Finally, have each child greet someone and exchange granola bars with that person.

When children have exchanged their Fish in the Sand bars, say: **Before we enjoy our tasty treats, let's say a prayer thanking God for other Christians and for the encouragement they give us.** Pray: **Dear God, thank you for giving us faithful Christian friends who help and encourage us. Please help each one of us to be an encouragement to others as well. Amen.**

If you have time, use graham crackers to make special Fish in the Sand treats for another class to encourage them as they learn about Jesus and his love.

MAKE WAY FOR JESUS!

OOD FOR THOUGHT

Jesus is the only way to God. *(John 14:6, 20, 21)*

IMPLE INGREDIENTS

You'll need Bibles, small paper cups, plastic spoons, a permanent marker, gumdrops, and prepared vanilla and lemon pudding.

Before class, use a permanent marker to write "John 14:6" at the bottom of each paper cup. Place a gumdrop at the bottom of each cup and spoon a layer of vanilla pudding over the gumdrop. Next, fill the cups with lemon pudding so no vanilla pudding is showing. Chill the parfaits before class.

EVOURING THE MESSAGE

Invite kids to form pairs and be sure each pair has a Bible. Then hand out the parfaits and plastic spoons. Say: **We all know that there's something at the bottom of these cups and that we need to find the right way to get to the bottom of the cups to discover what it is. In short, we have to go through the pudding that's on top! As you eat your pudding to discover the treasure at the bottom of the cup, chat about why you think Jesus is the way to God. After you discover the treasure, set your cup and spoon on the Bible.**

Allow several minutes for kids to discover the gumdrop and Scripture verse, then say: **What did you find when you went through the pudding? You found a nice treasure and an important Bible verse. Can someone look up that verse and read it aloud for us?** Allow a volunteer to read the verse, then read aloud John 14:20, 21 and ask:

- 🍎 **What did Jesus mean when he said he is the way to God?**
- 🍎 **How is Jesus "the truth and the life"?**

> ## TIDBITS
> Kids might enjoy learning that before early Christians were called Christians, they were known as "followers of the Way." After Jesus' death and resurrection, the disciples preached the Way to spread the good news about Jesus.

🍎 Are there any other ways to be with God? Explain.

🍎 Why is it important to know the only way to God is through Jesus?

Say: **Just as we went through the lemon pudding to reach the vanilla pudding, the gumdrop, and the Bible verse, we go through Jesus to find God. Jesus told us he is the way to God, the way to all truth, and the way to eternal life. When we know, love, and follow Jesus, we have the perfect way to the Father! In fact, Jesus is the only way to God! Jesus didn't say he was one way to God or that some people don't need to go through him. Jesus said that no one comes to the Father except through him. Wow! It feels great to know we have the truthful way to God and eternal life with him—all through Jesus!**

Ask for a volunteer to read aloud John 14:6 again. Then say: **Our spoons helped us go through the layer of pudding. What things help us be close to our way to God? In other words, how can we be close to Jesus and know him even better?** Encourage kids to name ways such as reading the Bible, praying, serving others, loving and obeying God, and going to church.

End with a prayer thanking Jesus for being the way to the Father and for giving us truth and eternal life. Challenge kids to make this special pudding parfait for their families and friends as powerful reminders that we must go through Jesus to be close to God.

LOVE THAT TASTE!

OOD FOR THOUGHT

Jesus wants us to love everyone—even our enemies. *(Matthew 5:44; Luke 6:27, 35)*

IMPLE INGREDIENTS

You'll need a Bible, paper plates, and a variety of foods children will love and dislike, such as fruits, crackers, small candies, spinach, anchovies, and lemons.

Before class, arrange the foods on a lazy Susan or large platter. Be sure that you have one of everything for each child and that you've included several foods kids won't relish! Three good-tasting and three bad-tasting foods should be enough.

DEVOURING THE MESSAGE

Place the selection of foods on a table and hand each child a paper plate. Instruct kids to choose one of each food item even if they don't like a particular item. Have children sit in a circle with the foods and taste each one as a group. Point out positive and negative reactions with comments such as "Wow! You all must like that one!" or "Ooo, I can see by your faces you don't care for that food."

When all the foods have been tasted, say: **I could tell that each of you has favorite foods and also ones you didn't care for. How is this like some of the people we know and how we react to them?**

Encourage kids to share their thoughts. Then say: **The people we come in contact with can create the same reactions we have with different foods. Some of them we really care for and enjoy being with, while others we might not like very much. But Jesus has some very important words about our likes and dislikes of people. Let's read what Jesus has to say.** Read aloud Matthew 5:44 and Luke 6:27, 35. Then ask:

🍎 Why does Jesus want us to love all people—even our enemies?

🍎 How does loving someone who may be unkind help change that person's attitudes and behavior?

🍎 How can we change the world by loving others? How does it change us?

🍎 What are things we can do to love others—even our enemies?

Say: **We can think of the foods we like as the nice people we know and love. And we can think of the foods we don't like as bullies, enemies, and others we don't enjoy. When Jesus tells us to love all people, he means that we are to love even those we might not like too much.**

Have kids take a bite of spinach or anchovy, then say: **It's not always easy to like everyone, is it? But it's important to obey Jesus and to love others—all others! You know, sometimes when we eat foods we don't like, we soon develop a taste for them and actually enjoy eating them! In the same way, we may discover that when we're kind to someone, we really enjoy the person who was hard to like at first! Now let's finish our snacks and try to enjoy even the ones that are hard to like.**

End by sharing a prayer asking Jesus' help in loving all people, even the most difficult to love. Challenge kids to think of one unlovable person to whom they can show love this week and see what changes come about.

JESUS FREES US!

OOD FOR THOUGHT

Jesus sets us free from sin and death. *(John 8:32; 14:6; Romans 8:1, 2)*

IMPLE INGREDIENTS

You'll need a Bible, small candy hearts, resealable plastic sandwich bags, ice-cube trays, straws, apple juice, and lemon-lime soda pop.

Before class, prepare the apple juice, then mix it with a bottle of lemon-lime soda pop. Fill ice-cube trays with the liquid, then drop a candy heart in one ice-cube square for each child. Freeze the cubes until solid. For each child, you'll need two "juice cubes" and one juice cube containing a candy heart.

EVOURING THE MESSAGE

Hand kids the plastic bags and straws. Invite children to place a juice cube containing a heart and two regular juice cubes in their plastic bags, then seal the bags tightly. Tell kids to hold the cubes to melt them and try to free the candy hearts.

As they hold their bags, say: **The hearts in our bags are trapped. They're surrounded and can't get out until they're freed. Before we knew Jesus, we were trapped, too. We were trapped by sin, by unkind acts, and even by death. That's not a very great place to be, is it? It made God sad to know we were trapped, and he wanted a way for us to be set free. Who did God send to free us from the trap of sin and death? Let's see!** Read aloud John 8:32; 14:6; and Romans 8:1, 2. Then ask:

🍎 **In what ways were we trapped before knowing and loving Jesus?**

🍎 **What happens when we live feeling trapped by the wrong things we do and say? How does being trapped by sin feel?**

🍎 **How can the truth set us free? Who is the Truth?** (Have kids read John 14:6 as a clue.)

🍎 **How was being set free by Jesus an amazing act of his love for us?**

In what ways does being set free allow us to serve Jesus more? love him more? love others more?

Say: **Being set free from sin, death, unkindness, stealing, and dishonesty is so wonderful! Being free means we're free to serve Jesus and show him our love. It means living our lives with the wonderful knowledge that we are God's friends and will have a place in heaven forever. And it means that we no longer are slaves to evil but can choose to do good, loving deeds instead! Jesus tells us that he is the Truth—and the truth can set us free! Wow! That's freedom!**

When the candy hearts are all freed, offer a prayer thanking Jesus for his love and forgiveness that set us free from sin and death. Then open the bags slightly and slide in the straws. Sip your chilled treats as you visit about ways our freedom in Christ helps us know, love, and follow Jesus more fully. Be sure to mention ways such as being free to pray, to ask Jesus for help, to trust God, to love others, and to have hope for eternal life.

Challenge kids to make these special juice cubes for friends and families and to explain how just as the candy hearts are set free, Jesus sets us free from sin and death.

TEMPTATION MONSTERS

OOD FOR THOUGHT

Jesus helps us overcome temptations. *(Matthew 4:1-11; Luke 22:39, 40; James 1:13, 14)*

IMPLE INGREDIENTS

You'll need a Bible, toothpicks, paper plates, plastic knives, softened strawberry cream cheese, small marshmallows, olives, and various vegetables such as carrots, celery, and cucumbers. You'll also need a small hard roll or baguette roll for each child.

Before class, clean and cut the vegetables into small shapes and pieces. Include the feathery tops of celery stalks and carrots (even parsley) in your vegetable collection. Carefully slice each roll halfway down its length.

EVOURING THE MESSAGE

Place the ingredients on a table and gather kids. Ask children to tell about a temptation they may have faced, such as skipping school, stealing a candy bar, or cheating on a test. Encourage kids to tell what they did with the temptation: whether they gave in and how they felt afterward, or whether they said no and how they felt.

After several kids share, say: **We've all faced temptations at some time in our lives. Temptations make us feel torn and uncomfortable and force us to make decisions about how we'll act. They're like little monsters snapping at our hearts and minds, trying to get us to do things we know may be wrong. Did you know that Jesus faced temptations? However, Jesus also knew that temptations to do wrong aren't from God, and he overcame being tempted! Let's see what Jesus did to overcome temptation.** Read aloud Matthew 4:1-11, then ask:

🍎 **Where did Jesus get the strength to say no and fight the temptations?**

🍎 **Where do you think temptations to do wrong come from?**

🍎 **How does trusting God and loving Jesus help us fight temptations? help us overcome evil?**

Say: **Jesus overcame temptations with his strength in God and with the power of God's Word! And we can devour the monster of temptation just as Jesus did, with God's strength, Jesus' love, and the power of God's Word. Let's make tempting treats right now, then gobble them down to remind us we can devour temptations through Jesus!**

Hand each child a sliced roll and a paper plate. Show kids how to spread cream cheese on the inside top and bottom of the sliced portion of roll. Poke a toothpick between the sliced portion of roll to make an open "mouth," then stick marshmallow teeth around the jaws. Spread cream cheese on the back of the Temptation Monsters and stick on vegetable bits. As children work, have them identify temptations they face, such as cheating, lying, stealing, skipping school or church, and gossiping. Finish your edible monsters by adding olive "eyes" stuck on with a bit of cream cheese.

When the Temptation Monsters are complete, read aloud Luke 22:39, 40 and James 1:13, 14. Then share a prayer asking God's help in overcoming temptations. After you pray, say: **God doesn't tempt us, though he may test us to see where our love and faith lie. We know that temptations to do wrong things aren't from God—and that's why we want to devour the Temptation Monster! As we devour our own edible temptations, let's brainstorm ways to overcome real-life temptations!** Suggest ways such as prayer, learning God's Word, allowing others to help us, and trusting in God's power and Jesus' love.

HUMBLE-JUMBLE

OOD FOR THOUGHT

Jesus wants us to have humble attitudes. *(Matthew 5:5; 2 Corinthians 10:18; Galatians 6:14)*

IMPLE INGREDIENTS

You'll need a Bible, napkins, a large paper grocery sack, paper bowls or sturdy muffin cups, a box of corn or wheat cereal flakes, and several boxes of fruity, sugar-coated cereal.

Before class, empty the cereals into the paper grocery sack and mix them up by shaking the bag. Be sure to choose one "plain" cereal and several colorful ones!

EVOURING THE MESSAGE

Place the grocery sack containing the cereal beside you and hand each child a napkin and a bowl or muffin cup. Invite kids to dip out some cereal in their containers, then sit in a circle. Tell kids not to eat the cereal yet!

Inform children that they are going to be cereal surveyors and you'd like to know their answers to a few questions. First, ask kids to tell which cereal flake or piece catches their eyes first and why. Responses will probably include "because of the color" or "it looks pretty." Have them place that piece of cereal on their napkins. Next, ask kids to identify which cereal looks like it would be the tastiest and why. Responses might include "because there are marshmallows on it" or "because it has a sugar coating." Place those cereal bits on the napkin. Now ask kids which cereal appears to be the most nutritious and pure—in other words, which is best for us without all the extra "stuff." Place those cereal pieces on the napkin.

Say: **Place the cereal pieces that seem to brag and say, "Look at me! I'm the best" to one side of your napkin. Is the plain cereal flake there? Why not?** Allow kids to tell their ideas, then continue: **The cereal that doesn't seem to shout "Look at me!" is probably the best cereal here for doing its job of feeding us and being nutritious. It doesn't brag about how great it is because it doesn't need to! We can think of the colored or sugar-coated cereals as braggers and the quiet but nutritious cereal as humble. Humble means we don't brag and show off or tell others how great we are. And being humble means we know there's someone much greater than we are!**

Jesus was very humble. He never bragged about his power or about being God's only Son. Instead, Jesus gave all the glory and credit to God, his Father! Wow! Just think how Jesus could have bragged if he had wanted to! And yet he didn't because Jesus knew humility is important! Let's see what Jesus and the Bible say about being humble. Read aloud Matthew 5:5; 2 Corinthians 10:18; and Galatians 6:14, then ask:

🍎 **Why is being humble better than being boastful? Which is more honest? Explain.**

🍎 **How are people who brag and want lots of attention like these cereals?**

🍎 **Why is bragging and being boastful puffed up and hollow?**

🍎 **In what ways does giving the glory and credit to God keep us humble? draw us nearer to God? keep us more honest?**

Then say: **Let's offer a prayer asking God to help us have humble attitudes and to give Jesus and God the glory and the credit for all things wise and wonderful! Each time you hear the words brag or boast, eat a sugar-coated cereal piece. Each time you hear the word humble, eat a humble cereal flake.** Pray: **Dear Lord, since we're human, we have a tendency to *brag* and *boast*. But we know that we are nothing when compared to your glory. We want to be *humble* and give you all the honor and glory. Please help us have *humble* attitudes. Amen.**

As kids crunch their cereal, have them take turns telling about times the Lord helped them or did something amazing for them. Then have everyone praise the Lord by saying, "Thank you, Lord, for your power!"

REMEMBRANCE MEAL

OOD FOR THOUGHT

Jesus teaches us to remember him. *(Luke 22:14-20; 1 Corinthians 11:24-26)*

IMPLE INGREDIENTS

You'll need a Bible, a loaf of French bread, paper cups, napkins, grape juice, endive (or chicory or another bitter herb), and dried pitted dates.

This edible object talk is perfect around Easter or any other time you want to remind children about Jesus' love or teach them about Communion at your church. Before class, prepare the grape juice or purchase ready-to-serve juice. If you want a more realistic seder, add cold lamb to the menu or serve some other meat to represent the lamb that was traditionally served.

EVOURING THE MESSAGE

Place a long table on the floor with its legs folded up. Set the grape juice, French bread, endive, and pitted dates in the center of the table. Set the table with napkins and paper cups. Be sure there's seating enough for each child. If your class is large, set two tables end to end on the floor.

Gather kids around the table on the floor. Say: **This is much the way that Jesus and his disciples would share meals. They would sit around a low table on mats and enjoy fruit, bread, meat, and wine. The women would usually serve the meal to the boys and men first, then enjoy their own special time later. One such supper was especially important because it was Jesus' last supper on earth. It was during Passover when the traditional seder supper was served. The seder, which included unleavened bread, lamb, bitter herbs, wine, and fruit, remembered the Israelites' plight and flight from Egypt. Let's learn about the special gift Jesus gave to us that night to remember him by as we share our own version of a seder supper.**

Pass the food items to each person, but save the bread and grape juice for later. Say: **Scripture was usually recited at this supper. Would anyone like to**

recite a Scripture verse they might know? Encourage kids to repeat several verses they might have memorized, or read aloud several verses from the Bible. Then say: **During their meal, Jesus picked up the cup of wine and told his disciples to share it, for it represented his blood that would be poured out for them.** Pour a bit of grape juice in each cup and let kids sip their juice. Say: **Then Jesus picked up the bread and gave thanks to God. Jesus broke the bread and told the disciples it was his body that was given to them and to eat it in remembrance of him.** Pass the bread and let kids each take a piece to munch.

Then say: **This was the Last Supper, but it was also the first Communion. Communion is the sharing of the bread and the cup that remind us of Jesus' loving sacrifice and how he gave of his blood and body when he died for our sins. It also reminds us that Jesus promises us a place in heaven with him when we accept him into our lives and hearts.** Read aloud Luke 22:14-20 and 1 Corinthians 11:24-26, then ask:

🍎 **In what ways was Jesus' gift of Communion like a special promise he gave us?**

🍎 **How is Jesus' gift of the bread and juice a demonstration of his love for us?**

🍎 **Jesus wants us to remember him. What things do you remember?**

Say: **Jesus wants us to remember him. But since we love Jesus so much, we want to do more than just remember; we want to honor and praise him. We want to love and obey him. And most of all, we want to invite Jesus into our hearts and lives. Communion is the remembrance of all Christ did for us through his love. Let's take a quiet moment to remember, then share a prayer thanking Jesus for his gift of love.**

Observe a few moments of silence, then pray: **Dear Lord, we thank you for your unbelievable love and sacrifice. We want to remember you not only in our minds but also in our hearts and through our actions and our words. We love you, Jesus. Amen.**

Invite a church leader into your classroom to talk about Communion and how it's celebrated at your church. Challenge kids to remember Jesus' sacrifice of love every day this week and to thank Jesus through their prayers.

LOVELY LIGHTS

OOD FOR THOUGHT

Jesus is the light of the world. *(John 8:12; Acts 13:47)*

IMPLE INGREDIENTS

You'll need a Bible, bananas, pineapple rings, confetti cake sprinkles, yellow jelly beans or gumdrops, paper plates, and plastic forks.

Before class, choose bananas that are not overly ripe. You'll need one banana for every two kids. You'll also need one fresh or canned pineapple ring for each child.

EVOURING THE MESSAGE

Place the ingredients on a table and pour the confetti sprinkles on a paper plate. Gather kids and ask them to name all the different types of lights they can think of and why each is helpful. Then say: **Lights help us find our way and stay safe. And they push away the darkness, too. How is this like what Jesus does for us?**

Allow time for kids to tell their ideas, then say: **Jesus is like a wonderful light who helps us find our way to God as we push away the darkness of sin. Jesus even said that he was the light of the world!** Read aloud John 8:12 and Acts 13:47, then ask:

🍎 **In what ways is Jesus a light for the world? How does he light up darkness?**

🍎 **In what kinds of ways does the light of Jesus help us?**

🍎 **What might it be like in the world without the light of Jesus' love and forgiveness?**

🍎 **How can we shine for Jesus? for others? for the world?**

Explain that you'll be making edible candles to remind kids that Jesus is the light of the world. Have kids each place a pineapple ring on a paper plate, then roll banana halves in the confetti sprinkles. Place the bananas upright on their flat ends in the pineapple rings as "candles." Finally, place a yellow jelly bean or gumdrop on top as the flame.

Before the candles are eaten, say: **Let's share a prayer thanking Jesus for being the light of the world and for helping us stay safe and in the light of his love. Hold your edible candles like special prayer candles as we pray.** Pray: **Dear Lord, thank you for shining your perfect light in our lives. Please let us shine your love to others. Amen.**

If there's time, let children decorate real candles to take home. Use white candles and a variety of pretty sewing pins with colorful knobs on the ends. Push the pins in the lower portions of the candles. Have kids place them on a saucer at home to light during dinner. After an adult lights the candle, have the entire family offer a prayer asking Jesus to help them carry the light of Jesus' love into the world. (Remind everyone to remove the pins as the candles burn down so the plastic balls won't melt.)

TURKISH DELIGHTS

OOD FOR THOUGHT

Jesus wants us to teach others about his love. *(Philippians 1:3-7; 1 Thessalonians 4:18; 5:11)*

IMPLE INGREDIENTS

You'll need a Bible, paper plates, plastic spoons, sandwich bags, granulated sugar, several pans of gelatin cubes, and fresh rose and carnation petals (available from florists).

Before class, gently wash and pat dry the rose and carnation petals. You'll want several flower petals for each child. Loosen the gelatin cubes so they can easily be spooned from the pan.

EVOURING THE MESSAGE

Have children sit in a circle and play a quick game of telephone by whispering the message, "Jesus wants us to tell others about his love!" When the message has completed its travels, have a volunteer repeat it. Then say: **Important messages are meant to be spread. That's why Jesus wants us to take his message of love and forgiveness around the world. After Jesus' death and resurrection, the disciples and others began traveling to tell others about Jesus. But it wasn't always easy. Some of these people were tossed into prison or even killed for their beliefs. But that didn't stop the spread of the gospel! Why do you think these early missionaries continued to travel and teach others about Jesus?**

After kids share their ideas, read aloud Philippians 1:3-7 and 1 Thessalonians 4:18; 5:11, then ask:

🍎 **Why is it important to spread the news about Jesus?**

🍎 **How does Jesus help us get the word out?**

🍎 **How are missionaries today like early missionaries who taught for Christ?**

🍎 **How can we help missionaries? How can we be missionaries for Jesus?**

Say: **One of the places the apostle Paul traveled was to the city of Ephesus, in what is now the country of Turkey. Paul stayed in Ephesus for two years and established a church there. In fact, one of the books of the Bible is called Ephesians because it contains Paul's teachings to that church. While there, Paul stayed with friends who helped support him by giving him a place to eat and sleep. He ate with them, prayed with them, and shared with them about Jesus. One of the foods Paul probably ate while in Ephesus is called Turkish Delight. Let's make Turkish Delights to remind us how a missionary brought the delight of Jesus to a city who had never known Christ before and how his friends helped Paul spread the Good News!**

> ## TIDBITS
> Kids might like to discover that, during Paul's day, Ephesus (in modern-day Turkey) was the fourth largest city in the Roman Empire and had the largest street in the world at that time: 36-feet wide and a 1/3 of a mile long!

Have half the kids spoon gelatin cubes onto plates while the other half shakes dampened flower petals in bags of sugar. Place several sugary flower petals on the gelatin cubes, then enjoy. As kids eat, have them brainstorm ways they can help and support missionaries or bring Jesus' truth to others as missionaries themselves. Point out that missionaries don't have to travel the world but can bring Jesus' love to others anywhere!

If there's time, have each child write a sentence or two telling about Jesus' love on a slip of paper. Then have kids spread out to deliver their mission-messages to

35

someone in church. When all the messages have been delivered, have children meet back in the classroom and share a prayer asking Jesus to help you either support or become missionaries, even if it's simply in your own church or neighborhood!

GiNGERBREAD HOUSES

OOD FOR THOUGHT

Jesus is our foundation for life! *(Matthew 7:24-27; 1 Corinthians 3:11)*

IMPLE INGREDIENTS

You'll need a Bible, graham crackers, tube icing, gumdrops, a can of cream-cheese frosting, plastic knives, pretzel sticks, paper plates, and tiny candy decorations such as cinnamon red hots, tiny flowers, and other shapes. You'll also need one small milk carton for each child.

Before class, pick up empty milk cartons from any grade-school cafeteria. Rinse and dry the cartons. Staple or tape the top of each carton together to form a "roof."

EVOURING THE MESSAGE

Hand each child a paper plate and a milk carton. Ask children what the shape of the cartons reminds them of, then encourage them to tell how houses are built, what materials seem best, and why it's important to lay good, strong foundations when we build. Lead kids to recognize that strong foundations can help houses stand when bad storms and earthquakes come along.

Then say: **Building our lives is a lot like building houses—we need to use only the best and strongest materials and foundations if we're to withstand the hardships life throws our way. Jesus taught about building our lives on a strong, sure foundation by telling a parable of two builders. Let's make nifty edible houses as we learn how Jesus wants us to build our lives.**

As you continue, have kids spread the sides of the milk cartons with a thick layer of cream-cheese frosting. **Say: Jesus told of two house builders. One built his house on sand, while the other built his on solid rock. What do you suppose happened when flooding rains came?**

Allow kids to tell their ideas, then hand each child six graham-cracker squares. Say: **The house on the sand washed away, while the house on the solid rock stood secure! Which was the wise builder and why?**

Let children tell their ideas as they place four graham-cracker walls on their houses, then spread frosting on the roof and place two more squares on the roof. Say: **Jesus wanted us to learn that when we build our lives on shaky things such as money, popularity, and pride, we will fall apart when troubles come against us. But when we build our lives on the firm foundation of Jesus, we can stand strong against any troubles!**

While kids use tube icing, pretzels, and the tiny candies to decorate their houses, read aloud 1 Corinthians 3:11. Explain that cornerstones are used to give identity to buildings and to show who they belong to. Have each child place a gumdrop corner-stone near the base of her edible house as a reminder that Jesus is our perfect cornerstone. Then ask:

🍎 **Why does Jesus want us to build our lives upon his love and forgiveness?**

🍎 **In what ways does loving and following Jesus provide our lives with a strong foundation?**

🍎 **What are some ways we can build our lives on Jesus?**

Encourage kids to mention reading the Bible, trusting Jesus, obeying God, and showing kindness as ways to build our lives on the firm foundation of Jesus.

When the houses are complete, have a quick "parade of homes" to display kids' delicious handiwork. Then read aloud Matthew 7:24-27. Say: **Building our houses with good materials and sturdy foundations is important. But building our lives on the strong foundation of Jesus is the best advice of all! Let's offer a prayer thanking Jesus for being our cornerstone and our strong foundation.** Have kids hold their houses as they pray: **Dear Lord, thank you for loving us and for helping us build our lives on you. Amen.**

Encourage kids to show their houses to family and friends and to explain that Jesus is our cornerstone and perfect foundation for life!

HEAVEN AND EARTH

OOD FOR THOUGHT

Jesus is the bridge between God and people. *(John 14:6; 17:20-23, 26)*

IMPLE INGREDIENTS

You'll need a Bible, paper plates, plastic forks and knives, peeled cooked potatoes, apple wedges, cinnamon-sugar, butter, and an electric skillet. If you choose to make the poster-board bridge (see below), you will also need poster board, tape, and markers.

Before class, cook and peel several potatoes, but don't cut them. Wash and dry several apples, then cut them into wedges. For a colorful touch, use green, yellow, and red apples!

EVOURING THE MESSAGE

Preheat the electric skillet on medium-high. Keep the skillet out of kids' reach until you're ready to prepare the snack.

Invite kids to sit or lie on the floor and make bridges by pushing up off the ground with their feet and hands. As kids are in their bridge formations, say: **You look like bridges! You're spanning the distance between where your feet are and where your hands touch the floor! You're bridging from one place to another. All right, bridges, slowly come down, then sit upright. Bridges are helpful when we need to get from one place to another. We have bridges over lakes and streams, bridges over busy highways, and bridges over railroad tracks. But there's a much more important bridge than any of these—a bridge between heaven and earth! Who do you think might be the bridge between heaven and earth?**

Allow kids to tell their ideas, then say: **Jesus is that special bridge! Jesus came to earth as God's Son to bridge the gap between God and us, between heaven and earth. The Bible tells us that Jesus was fully human, yet he was fully God. That means that Jesus knew how and what we feel and how and what God feels, too. Jesus is our intercessor; that means that we can go to Jesus when we**

have troubles or fears or worries—and he knows how we feel and how to help us. Jesus intercedes for us with God. In other words, Jesus bridges the gap between humans and God, heaven and earth! Let's make a delicious snack called Heaven and Earth to remind us how Jesus is the bridge that joins God and us. Potatoes are from the ground so they can represent the earth, and apples are up high so they'll represent heaven.

Have half the kids cut the cooked potatoes into slices or pieces and the other half cut thin apple slices. Melt two tablespoons of butter in the electric skillet. Then put the potatoes and apples in the skillet and cook for several minutes. As the food cooks, read aloud John 14:6; 17:20-23, 26. Then ask:

🍎 What would it be like if we had no bridge to heaven or to God?

🍎 How was Jesus' role as our special bridge difficult for him? wonderful for him?

🍎 How can we help others know Jesus is the only bridge between us and God?

After the snacks cook for several minutes, sprinkle them with cinnamon-sugar and spoon them on paper plates. Before eating, share a prayer thanking Jesus for being the mighty bridge between heaven and earth.

If there's time, cut a sheet of poster board in half lengthwise, then tape the pieces together to make one long strip. Challenge kids to use markers to write words that describe what Jesus does as our bridge, such as healing us, helping us, calming our fears, understanding our feelings, and loving us. Then tape the ends of the poster board to the floor in the shape of a bridge for others to read and enjoy.

THE SWEETEST PROMISE

OOD FOR THOUGHT

Jesus was God's promise fulfilled. *(Isaiah 7:14; 9:6; Luke 2:8-20)*

IMPLE INGREDIENTS

You'll need a Bible, animal crackers, chow mein noodles, and a candy cane for each child.

DEVOURING THE MESSAGE

Have kids form pairs. Hand each child a candy cane and have children unwrap the top portion but not eat the candy yet. Ask kids what time of year they see candy canes in the stores and what holiday the striped candy is associated with. Then say: **Candy canes are so beautiful—they really are the Christmas candy! Let's use our candy canes to retell the story of God's most wonderful promise and how it was kept. Follow along with your candy canes!**

TiDBiTS

Kids might like knowing that a candy maker in Indiana invented the candy cane. He wanted a staff-shaped candy to remind people how shepherds came to honor our Savior. He also used red and white stripes as reminders of the price Jesus paid for our sins.

Shepherds with their staffs were in the fields. *(Hold it like a staff.)* **They were watching their flocks in the still of the night when an angel came down from heaven to them.** *(Roll the candy cane between your palms to make it flutter.)* **The angel told the shepherds not to be afraid, then said, "I bring you good news of great joy that will be for all the people. Today in the town of David a Savior has been born to you; he is Christ the Lord. This will be a sign to you: You will find a baby wrapped in cloths and lying in a manger." Then there was heavenly music** *(play a pretend trumpet),* **and the angels praised God!**

The shepherds smiled with joy *(hold the candy cane up like a smile on your face)* **and hurried to find the special baby God had promised the world.** *(Pretend to use the canes to walk.)* **They looked at a bright star that led their way** *(pretend to look through a candy-cane telescope),* **and soon they came to a small stable. They heard animal sounds coming from inside. There was a cow with a curly horn** *(hold the candy canes on your head),* **a feathery rooster who sang in the morn** *(flutter the candy canes like feathers),* **and a horse that neighed, "A baby's been born!" Finally, there, lying in the manger** *(hold the candy cane sideways to make a manger),* **was the special child God promised. The child who was pure like the white of our candy. The child who would grow up, then shed his blood, like the red of our candy, for our sins. The child who would be whipped for our sins with stripes on his back, like the stripes we see on our candy canes. Who was this special baby the shepherds wanted to meet? The "J" is for Jesus** *(hold the candy canes upside down to make the letter J)*—**so perfectly sweet!** *(Have partners place their candy canes together to make heart shapes.)*

Have kids enjoy licking their candy canes as you read aloud Isaiah 7:14 and 9:6. Then ask:

🍎 **In what ways is Jesus God's perfect promise to us?**

How is Jesus a promise in our own lives? in the lives of others around the world?

How can we thank God for his gift of Jesus?

Say: **Candy canes remind us of God's perfect promise, who was Jesus. The shape, the colors, even the letter J that stands for Jesus' name. As you enjoy the rest of your candy cane, give thanks for God's perfect promise with each sweet taste and remember the sweetness of Jesus!** Have partners make heart shapes once more with their candy canes, then offer a prayer thanking God for his gift of Jesus and his promise of love and salvation that was kept with Jesus' birth.

PRECIOUS PENNY SOUP

OOD FOR THOUGHT

Jesus teaches us to share what we have. *(Mark 12:41-44; 2 Corinthians 8:3; 9:7; Hebrews 13:16)*

IMPLE INGREDIENTS

You'll need a Bible, paper cups, plastic spoons, an electric skillet, oyster crackers, several cans of clear beef broth, and a shiny penny for each child plus one extra.

A week before class, send a note home with kids asking them to each bring a cooked and chopped vegetable to share with the class. (You may wish to bring in extra vegetables in case someone forgets.) Scrub and rinse one of the shiny pennies with rubbing alcohol or hydrogen peroxide. Keep that penny separate from the others to add to the Penny Soup.

EVOURING THE MESSAGE

Fill the electric skillet half full of water and pour in the clear broth. Place the other ingredients, cups, and spoons on the table. Have kids hold their contributions and gather around the table. Hold up the shiny penny and say: **This penny doesn't seem like much money, does it? And no one would ever believe this penny could help feed our entire class! But we're going to learn about sharing and how even a little can go a long way. You've each brought food to share and though not one of you has enough to feed the whole class, you'll see how sharing a little means—and makes—a lot! Listen as I tell you about a time Jesus taught about sharing what we have.**

Say: **One day Jesus was in Jerusalem at the temple, watching people come to offer money at the temple. Many rich people were putting much money into the offering. But a poor widow came and dropped in two small copper coins— less than a penny's worth.** Drop the penny into the electric skillet.

Continue: **After the poor widow gave her coins, Jesus told his disciples that the poor woman had given more than the rich people had. Why do you think he said that?** Encourage kids to tell their ideas, then say: **Jesus explained that the wealthy people gave out of their abundance and wouldn't even miss their coins but that the poor woman had little to give but gave everything she had. What else does God say about giving and sharing with others? Let's find out!** Read aloud 2 Corinthians 8:3; 9:7 and Hebrews 13:16, then ask:

- 🍎 **Why is it important to give and share what you can?**
- 🍎 **What are things we can give to help others?**
- 🍎 **How can sharing or giving even a small amount help?**

Then have the children carefully drop the vegetables they have into the "offering" skillet. Let kids take turns stirring the Penny Soup. Say: **When we have only a small amount to share or give, it's important that we still share it. Jesus wants us to know that how much we give isn't important—it's the way we feel when we give and share with others that counts! When each person shares what he can, there's a whole potful of blessings to go around! You shared small amounts of food today, but now we have a big potful of delicious Penny Soup to go around.**

Before serving the soup, share a prayer asking Jesus to help you remember to give what you can even if it seems small or insignificant, then thank him for the blessings he gives us. Spoon soup into everyone's cup, being careful not to spoon the penny into anyone's cup. Let kids drop oyster-cracker "coins" into their Penny Soup.

Close by handing each child a shiny penny to pass along to a friend or a family member as a reminder to give and share what we can to help others. See how many people the pass-along-pennies can reach with Jesus' message of sharing!

WHITE AS SNOWBALLS

OOD FOR THOUGHT

Jesus cleans us white as snow. *(Isaiah 1:18; Hebrews 10:22; 2 Peter 1:9)*

IMPLE INGREDIENTS

You'll need a Bible, sturdy spoons, a bowl and a spoon, 1 cup powdered sugar, 1/4 cup cottage cheese, 1/2 cup cream cheese, paper plates, and damp paper towels.

Before class, soften the cream cheese. This recipe makes about ten snowballs, so adjust it according to your class size.

EVOURING THE MESSAGE

Place the ingredients on a table and gather kids. Ask kids to tell things that need to be cleaned, such as dirty shoes, hands after playing, and grass-stained clothes. Then ask children how it feels to wear clothes that are messy and unclean.

Say: **Think for a moment about how you'd feel if you fell into a mud puddle. You'd be covered with dirt, and your clothes and hair would feel awful! How would you get clean? By taking a bath and washing your clothes. Then, ah, you'd feel fresh as snow and just like new! Did you know that the Bible says our hearts and lives are as unclean as falling into a mud puddle? Romans 3:23 says that all of us have sinned and fallen short of the glory of God. That means that we've all done and said things that make us unclean and stained and that keep us from God. But hopping in the bath won't make us clean from sin.**

There's only one person who can do that kind of super cleaning—Jesus! Let's read what Jesus can do for us and how he can make us clean and fresh as snow. Read aloud Isaiah 1:18; Hebrews 10:22; and 2 Peter 1:9. Then ask:

 Why did we need God to send someone to make us clean and white as snow—in other words, to take away our sins?

 In what ways does sin keep us unclean and far away from God?

 How does Jesus make us clean and new, as white as snow?

 What changes happen in our lives when we're made fresh and new?

Say: **Just as new fallen snow makes everything clean, fresh, and new, Jesus makes us clean and new with his love and forgiveness. Jesus came to die for our sins so we could be clean and live closer to God. When we ask Jesus into our lives and promise to love and follow him, the stains of sin are removed and we're washed clean and white as snow! Let's make edible snowballs that will help remind us that when Jesus removes our sins, we're washed white as snow!**

Have children cream together the softened cream cheese and the cottage cheese. Pour the powdered sugar on a paper plate. Hand each child a spoonful of the cheese mixture to form a sticky ball, then roll it in powdered sugar to make a sweet snowball. If you have enough cheese, invite each child to make two scrumptious snowballs. Provide damp paper towels for cleanup.

End by forming a very close circle and having kids bow their heads and close their eyes. Softly say: **If you've ever said an unkind word, take a step backward.** Pause. **If you've ever acted unkindly, take a step backward.** Pause. **If you've ever forgotten to pray, take a step backward.** Pause. **And if you've ever thought a mean thought, take another step backward.** Pause. **This is how far sin takes us from God, step by step, until we're too far to be near him.**

Pause, then say: **But Jesus' love and forgiveness bring us close to God by changing us and making us white as snow. Now, if you have ever thought a nice thought, take a step forward.** Pause. **If you've ever prayed for someone, take a step forward.** Pause. **If you've ever done something to help someone, take a step forward.** Pause. **And if you've ever said a kind word, take another step forward. This is how close we feel to God when we're cleaned with Jesus' love and forgiveness. Thank you, Jesus, for living and dying and living again so that we could be washed clean and white as snow. Amen.**

Challenge kids to make these delicious snowballs to remind their families and friends that when we ask for Jesus' forgiveness and accept him into our lives, we are washed clean and white as snow.

44

JoLLY JeLLY BeaNS

OOD FOR THOUGHT

Jesus died for us and is alive again! *(Isaiah 53:5; Romans 5:6-10)*

IMPLE INGREDIENTS

You'll need a Bible, several bags of jelly beans, small plastic sandwich bags, colored rubber bands, several bowls, and copies of the poem from page 47.

Use this object talk around Easter or sometime in the spring. Before class, make two or three photocopies of the poem on page 47 for each child. Cut out the poem boxes. Be sure you have plenty of jelly beans! You may wish to use plastic pull-apart Easter eggs instead of plastic bags and rubber bands.

EVOURING THE MESSAGE

Put the jelly beans in several bowls and have children sit around the bowls. Hand each child a plastic sandwich bag (or pull-apart Easter egg). Say: **We usually think of Easter when we see jelly beans, but what does Easter make us think of? Many people think only of jelly beans or other candies they'll find in their Easter baskets. They don't stop to remember the real reason for the season—Jesus! But you can think of the stone that was rolled away from Jesus' tomb when you see jelly beans, or maybe you can use these colorful beans as reminders of the Easter story. As I read a poem, choose a jelly bean of each color I mention and place it in your bag.**

Read the poem on page 47, allowing children to put a jelly bean of each color in their bags. After all the jelly beans are in the bags, hand each child a copy of the poem and a colored rubber band. Slide the poems in the bags and attach the rubber bands to hold the jelly beans inside.

Let children nibble extra jelly beans from the bowls as you read aloud Isaiah 53:5 and Romans 5:6-10. Then ask:

🍎 **How did Jesus demonstrate his love for us when he died on the cross?**

🍎 How does it feel to know that Jesus is alive and offers us forgiveness and eternal life in heaven?

🍎 How can we thank and praise Jesus for the great sacrifice he made for us?

Say: **Jesus was part of God's plan for our salvation. That means that Jesus came to love us, teach us, and forgive us through dying on the cross for our sins. But God's plan didn't stop there! Jesus was risen after three days and is alive and helping us right now. When we ask Jesus to live in our hearts and love and follow him, he promises us eternal life, too! Now that's something to be happy about! Let's share a prayer thanking Jesus for his gift of eternal life, then we'll make an Easter story jelly-bean bag to share with friends.**

Pray: **Dear Lord, there are not words to thank you enough for the great price you paid to free us from sin and death. Your love is more than we can ever understand! Thank you for loving us and for fulfilling God's plan to give us eternal life. Amen.**

Finish by having each child make one or two more bags to share with someone during the week. Tell kids to be sure and remind everyone that Jesus died for our sins but is alive so we can have eternal life.

THE COLORS OF LOVE

Yellow is for God's only Son,
who came here to love us—every one.
Black is the color of our sin
and how we all felt when they crucified him.
Red is for blood shed on the cross
and for our hearts broken from such a great loss.
Orange is the sunset as he lay in the tomb
and for the great stone that sealed the room.
Pink is for sunrise on the third day,
when Mary and her friends came to the grave.
White is the angel who caused them such fear
but said, "Jesus is risen. He's no longer here!"
Green is the color of eternal life
that Jesus has bought us and paid with his life.
Purple is for his heavenly reign—
and forever we'll praise him and honor his name!